HOW
TO BE A
MATHEMAGICIAN

ADITI SINGHAL

SUDHIR SINGHAL

HOW

TO BE A

MATHEMAGICIAN

EBURY
PRESS

EBURY PRESS

USA | Canada | UK | Ireland | Australia
New Zealand | India | South Africa | China

Ebury Press is part of the Penguin Random House group of companies
whose addresses can be found at global.penguinrandomhouse.com

Published by Penguin Random House India Pvt. Ltd
7th Floor, Infinity Tower C, DLF Cyber City,
Gurgaon 122 002, Haryana, India

First published in Ebury Press by Penguin Random House India 2017

Copyright © Aditi Singhal and Sudhir Singhal 2017
Illustrations by M. Saquib

ISBN 9780143427483

Typeset in Adobe Garamond Pro by Manipal Digital Systems, Manipal
Printed at Replika Press Pvt. Ltd, India

www.penguin.co.in

CONTENTS

PART B: FUN WITH NUMBERS

INTRODUCTION

Magic holds a strange fascination for kids and grown-ups alike. On the other hand, maths is something that invokes fear in many. A magician's tricks tend to amaze us and push our brains into overdrive, trying to discover how the trick was performed, whereas tricky maths equations create a mental block. This book is an attempt to draw out the similarities between maths and magic and, in the process, make you fall in love with numbers.

This section of the book contains magic tricks and other fun-filled activities. The speciality of the tricks taught in this book is that you can perform them anywhere, at any given time, and entertain yourself, your friends and family. You can use these in classrooms, parties, at work or even while travelling. By mastering these tricks, you will be able to give people the impression that you can read their minds or do calculations faster than a computer. The other section of this book (just flip the book around to find it!) contains mathematical facts, calculation tips, maths problems and even teaches you some tricks to improve your concentration.

To perform the tricks given in this book your main prop will be you. For some of the tricks, you might need some basic things, such as a pen, a sheet of paper and a deck of cards.

Some of the secrets in each section of the book will amaze you, and we are sure that after reading this book you will have a fresh perspective on mathematics. We wish you luck as you embark on the journey to become a mathemagician.

PART A

MAGIC WITH MATHS

1

MATHS TELEPATHY

Wouldn't it be wonderful if you could read other person's mind? Let's learn a trick to predict a number flashing in someone else's mind and make everyone believe that you are a mind reader. We call it maths telepathy!

All you need is:
   – A paper
   – A pen

MAGIC TRICK 1

Step 1
Ask a person in the audience to write down a three- or four-digit number with distinct digits, i.e. without repeating any number. For example, 2684.

Step 2

Tell them to multiply this number by any single-digit number, other than zero. Say, 2684 × 6 = 16104.

Step 3

Tell them to multiply the result with another single-digit number. Say, 16104 × 3 = 48312.

Step 4

Tell them to write a number formed by rearranging the digits of the answer, in any order: For example, 48312 can become 81324 or 48123 or 32184 or 31248, etc. Let's take 83124.

Step 5

Ask them to consider the numbers obtained in step 3 and step 4, and subtract the smaller number from the larger one. In the above example, it should be 83124 − 48312 = 34812.

Step 6

Ask them to circle any one of the digits from the answer, other than zero.

Say, they circled 4 in 3 ④ 8 1 2

Step 7

Now you say:

'I don't know which number you selected in the beginning and which numbers you multiplied it with.

'Just concentrate on the number you have circled.

'Now tell me the digits of the number that you didn't circle, slowly one by one and in any order.'

Step 8
The person tells you the digits they did not circle, say 3. . . 1 . . . 8 . . . 2.

Listening to these digits and applying the magic you will be able to guess that the encircled number is '4'.

A magician never reveals his or her secrets, but we, as educationists, believe that knowledge increases by sharing.

MATHS BEHIND THE MAGIC 1

Let us understand the secret that will empower you to guess the circled number even without knowing any of the numbers that the person has thought of in their mind.

1. The trick lies in the end when the user tells you the remaining digits, which they did not encircle. All you have to do then is to add all those digits in your mind. In the above example, it will be 3 + 1 + 8 + 2 = 14.
2. If the answer is more than 9, add the digits of the number again until you get a single-digit number. Say the answer after adding the digits in above example is 14, then add 1 + 4 = 5.
3. Subtract this final number from 9 and you will get the encircled number, i.e. 9 – 5 = 4. *Magic!*
4. When you take any number and subtract it from the number obtained after changing the position of its digits, the result is always a multiple of 9.
5. For any random number the user takes, you have to follow the first three steps to get the circled digit.

To see more general proof, refer to Chapter 3: 'Trick to Impress Anyone'.

2

MAGIC USING THE DICTIONARY

In this trick, we will learn some magic that involves using not just numbers but also a dictionary full of words. We use this trick in many of our sessions.

All you need is:
- A paper
- A pen
- A dictionary

MAGIC TRICK 2

Step 1
Ask one person from the audience to write down any three-digit number (all the digits should be distinct, i.e. without repeating any digit) on a piece of paper and not show it to anyone.

Step 2
Then ask them to reverse the digits to form a new number and subtract the smaller number from the larger one.

Step 3

Now ask them to open the dictionary to the page corresponding to the number obtained in Step 2 and look up the fourth word on that page.

Step 4

Ask them to tell you the first letter of that word and close the dictionary.

Step 5

Now bring the dictionary to your ears as if it is whispering the word to you and magically reveal that word!

Everyone will be amazed and will wonder if you were really talking to the dictionary or if you could read a person's mind.

MATHS BEHIND THE MAGIC 2

The logic lies in the following:

The difference between a three-digit number and its reverse is always a multiple of nine.*

So, you have only nine possible answers as page numbers, they are:
page 99, page 198, page 297, page 396, page 495, page 594, page 693, page 792 or page 891.

Just memorize the fourth word on these pages (i.e. only nine words) and do the magic.

*To see a more detailed algebraic proof, read Chapter 3.

3

TRICK TO IMPRESS ANYONE

Once we conducted a workshop for teachers from various prominent schools of Mumbai. Almost all the teachers shared the concern that most students fear algebra. Although they understand the topic, they do not find it interesting. I remembered a magic trick that relied heavily on algebra without seeming to. I decided to show it to them so that they could understand how teaching algebra can be made enjoyable by linking it to day-to-day concepts.

I took a piece of paper and scribbled a word on it. Then I folded it and gave it to one of the teachers. Everyone was curious about what was going to happen next.

MAGIC TRICK 3

Step 1
I asked that teacher to give me a random three-digit number with distinct digits. She said, '725,' and I wrote it on the board.

Step 2

I asked her to pass on that folded piece of paper to another teacher. I told this next teacher to tell me the number we get from reversing the digits of the previous number. '527,' she replied. I wrote it down below the first number.

Step 3

The paper was then passed on to another teacher, and he was asked to calculate the difference between the two given numbers.

'198,' he replied.

Step 4

Now as the paper was passed on to another teacher, she was asked to give the number obtained by reversing the digit of this new number. '891,' she replied.

Step 5

I wrote 891 under 198 and asked everyone to add the two.

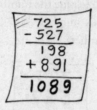

At this point, I told one of the teachers sitting in the front row to open the book on my table. I had used this book earlier to explain some concepts to them. She was asked to go to page 108 and to read out the ninth word of the first line.

'We,' she said.

Then I asked the teacher who had the folded piece of paper in her hand to open it and read aloud the word scribbled on it. 'We,' she said.

Everyone in the room was astounded. They all wanted to know how I knew the word even before the teachers gave me random numbers.

'Well, it's the magic trick of algebra.' I smiled.

MATHS BEHIND THE MAGIC 3

Let us understand the trick using algebra.

Step 1
Let us denote the three digits of the three-digit number as a, b and c. Then keeping the place value in mind, we can say that the three-digit number would be:

$$100a + 10b + c$$

Step 2
The number obtained by reversing the three digits is:

$$100c + 10b + a$$

Step 3
Subtracting the smaller number from the larger number, we get:

$$100a + 10b + c$$
$$- \underline{(100c + 10b + a)}$$
$$99a - 99c$$
$$\text{Or } 99(a - c)$$

Since, a and c are distinct single-digit numbers, the possible values of $(a - c)$ are:
1, 2, 3, 4, 5, 6, 7, 8 or 9
And the only possible results of their product with 99 are:
099, 198, 297, 396, 495, 594, 693, 792 or 891

When you add any of these numbers with the reverse of itself, you will always get 1089.

4

GIVING THE ANSWER BEFORE
KNOWING THE QUESTION

L et's learn a simple but amazing trick that leaves everyone flabbergasted. We often use this trick in our workshops and seminars as a curtain-raiser. It always results in the same response, that of amazement and disbelief.

All you need is:
  – A small piece of paper
  – A pen

MAGIC TRICK 4

Step 1
On a small piece of paper, write a seven-digit number, say 2545767. Fold this paper and give it to someone sitting in the front row in the audience or one of your friends. Tell them not to open it till they are asked to do so.

Step 2

Begin by saying, 'Let's start the magic by writing some random six-digit number,' and write a number on the board or on another paper or a notebook. Let's say it is 345769.

Step 3

Ask someone from the audience or your friend to tell any six-digit number and write it below the number written in step 2. Let's say that the person gives 762014.

Step 4

Now you write one more six-digit number below these two numbers, say 337985.

Step 5

You can ask the same person or another person to give one more six-digit number and write it below the written numbers. Let's say they give 185637.

Step 6

Finally, you write another six-digit number below these four numbers, say 914362.

Step 7

Ask the audience or your friends to add these five numbers and write the total at the bottom, which, in this case, is 2545767.

Step 8

Now tell the person you gave the slip of paper in the beginning to open it and reveal the number written on it.

Everyone will see that the number written on that paper is the same as the total of these five numbers, i.e. 2545767.

Special Tip

This trick will work with any number of digits, so you are not limited to a six-digit numbers. You may start with a five-digit or ten-digit number or even higher to perform this trick. But remember that the number of digits should be the same for all numbers.

MATHS BEHIND THE MAGIC 4

1. The first step is to think of any six-digit number in your mind, such as 345769 in the above example. Now you have to do a simple and quick calculation.

2. Add '22' to the first digit of your number. Here it is 3, so 3 + 22 = 25.

3. Now subtract 2 from the last digit. Here it is 9, so 9 – 2 = 7.

4. Let the other digits remain.

5.

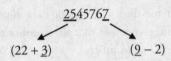

$$2545767$$

$$(22 + \underline{3}) \qquad\qquad (\underline{9} - 2)$$

This is the number that you are going to write on a piece of paper and give to someone in the audience and it will be the final answer.

6. On the board, write the first six-digit number that you thought of, in this case 345769.

7. Ask someone from the audience or your friend to give a six-digit number below yours. In this case we assume that the person gave 762014.

8. Now it's your turn to write another six-digit number below it, making it appear to be just a random number. However, actually it is *not*. To write the new number you have to subtract the first digit of the number given by the other person from 10 and subtract all other digits from 9.

```
  1 0 9 9 9 9
 – 7 6 2 0 1 4        ⟶   friend's number
    3 3 7 9 8 5        ⟶   your new number
```

9. Again ask for one more random number from the audience, 185637 in this case.

10. Repeat the previous calculation to give your next number as shown below:

```
 10 9 9 9 9 9
 − 1 8 5 6 3 7        ──────────→   friend's number
   9 1 4 3 6 2        ──────────→   your new number
```

11. Finally, ask the audience to add all the five numbers to get the answer as 2545767. And ask the person holding your slip of paper to reveal the number written by you before you begun and show that you knew the answer before the question. *Magic!*

Now let's discover how it works:

- Actually, the number you had written after the audience's number was arrived at by deducting the first digit from 10 and rest from 9, so the sum of the audience's number and the one given by you will become 1099999,
  i.e. 762014 + 337985 = 1099999 and
  185637 + 914362 = 1099999

- So, we already knew that we are adding '1099999 + 109999 = 2199998' to our initial number, or we can say '2200000 − 2'. That's why we added '22' to the first digit and subtracted '2' from the last digit of our initial number to get the total sum in advance.

```
            3 4 5 7 6 9  ──────→  your initial number
          ┌ 7 6 2 0 1 4  ──────→  audience number
1099999  ┤
          └ 3 3 7 9 8 5  ──────→  your number
          ┌ 1 8 5 6 3 7  ──────→  audience number
1099999  ┤
          └ 9 1 4 3 6 2  ──────→  your number
            2 5 4 5 7 6 7  ─────→  Total
```

5

THE MAGICAL CARDS

A deck of cards is an amazing prop/tool used by magicians and illusionists in many different ways. We too can't resist sharing a trick or two with playing cards. In this magic trick, you will learn how you can predict the card chosen by another person without even looking at it.

Material required:
   – A deck of cards
   – A calculator (optional)

MAGIC TRICK 5

Step 1
Take a deck of cards and shuffle it two or three times or ask someone in the audience to come and do it for you.

Step 2

Now you can ask the same person or someone else to select any card from that deck. Ask them to check it. If it is a face card (i.e. jack, queen, king) or the number 10, they will have to pick another card. (This trick can only be played with cards numbered 1–9, where the ace is considered 1). Once your volunteer has a number card, ask them to keep the card and show it to no one.

Let's suppose the chosen card was the '7 of spades'.

Step 3

Now you also take one card from the deck and make sure only you know your card and no one else can see it. In case you get a face card or the number 10, select another one. Let's say you got the '4 of clubs'.

Step 4

Ask your volunteer to mentally multiply their card number by *2*. In this example it will be:

$$7 \times 2 = 14$$

Step 5

Ask them to add 2 to the answer.

$$14 + 2 = 16$$

Step 6

Now ask them to multiply the newly obtained answer by 5.

$$16 \times 5 = 80$$

Step 7
Then ask to subtract 6 from the new number.
$$80 - 6 = 74$$

Step 8
Finally ask your volunteer to show their chosen card to the audience. Place your card next to that card. Your volunteer's card will be the first digit of the final number and your card will be the second digit. He or she will see that the number formed is actually the final answer given by them. *Magic!*

Special Tip

You can call one or two people on stage to perform this magic or involve all participants if it is a small group. You can also ask them to just visualize any card in their mind other than jack, queen, king and 10, instead of choosing a card from the deck.

MATHS BEHIND THE MAGIC 5

Let us understand how the final answer came out as a combination of your and the other person's cards.

1. As mentioned earlier, we play this trick only with cards numbered 1 to 9.
2. Then we ask the participant to multiply the card number by 2 and then add 2 to the result.
$$(7 \times 2) + 2$$
3. Then the participant is supposed to multiply the new number by 5. So actually, we are multiplying the number by 10(first by 2 and then by 5). Here it was $7 \times 10 = 70$.
4. We also added 2 in between which is also multiplied by 5 in the next step, which means we are adding 10 more to the number, as in our example it was :
$$(7 \times 2 \times 5) + (2 \times 5)$$
$$70 + 10 = 80$$
5. Now finally we ask the participant to subtract a number from his final answer. This number is actually the magic trick. It is not a fixed number that you can use in all situations, but will change according to *your* card number. You have to choose this number by subtracting your card number from 10. In the given example, your card number is 4, so this magic number would be '$10 - 4 = 6$'. Subtracting this number, i.e. 6, from 80 gives 74 as final answer.

Audience card: 7

Your card: 4

Steps done by participant:

Step 1	$7 \times 2 = 14$	⟶ card number × 2
Step 2	$14 + 2 = 16$	⟶ result of Step 1 + 2
Step 3	$16 \times 5 = 80$	⟶ result of Step 2 × 5
Step 4	$80 - 6 = 74$	⟶ result of Step 3 – magic number

(10 – 'magic number')

6

MAGIC SUM

This 'Magic Sum' trick is absolutely amazing and we are sure you are going to love it.

All you need is:
- Two sheets of paper
- A pen or a pencil

MAGIC TRICK 6

Step 1
On a piece of a paper, make a table with four rows and four columns and write the numbers 1 to 16, as shown below:

1	2	3	4
5	6	7	8
9	10	11	12
13	14	15	16

Step 2

Tell your audience that you are going to write down the final answer even before you begin. On another small piece of paper, write 'The sum of the four circled numbers is 34', fold it a few times and keep it aside.

Step 3

Ask a person from the audience to come and circle any number on the table. See the example shown in the figure.

1	2	3	4
5	6	⑦	8
9	10	11	12
13	14	15	16

Step 4

Ask them to cross out all the numbers in the same column and row of the number that they circled.

1	2	3̶	4
5̶	6̶	⑦	8̶
9	10	11̶	12
13	14	15̶	16

Step 5

Ask the person to circle any of the remaining numbers, i.e. which is neither circled nor crossed out.

1	2	3̶	4
5̶	6̶	⑦	8̶
⑨	10	11̶	12
13	14	15̶	16

Step 6

Ask them to repeat Step 4, i.e. to cross out all the numbers in the column and row to which this newly circled number belongs.

1̶	2	3̶	4
5̶	6̶	⑦	8̶
⑨	10̶	11̶	12̶
13̶	14	15̶	16

Step 7

Instruct your volunteer to repeat steps 5 and 4 until you are left with four numbers circled and all the others are crossed out.

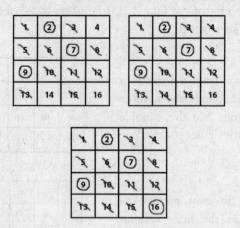

Step 8

Finally ask them to add the four circled numbers.

$$2 + 7 + 9 + 16 = 34$$

Unfold the piece of paper on which you had written your prediction, which says 'The sum of four circled numbers is 34', and reveal it to the audience.

MATHS BEHIND THE MAGIC 6

Let's see how we can predict the sum of the circled numbers:

Whenever you make an array of consecutive numbers, the sum of the four circled numbers, as per the directions given in the trick, will always be the sum of the numbers of either of the two diagonals.

Every combination of four numbers entails picking no two in the same row or column, i.e. when you transpose the columns of two numbers in different rows, you add and subtract the same distance to the diagonal. Thus the total sum remains the same as the sum of the diagonal.

Hence, in our example, the numbers in one of the diagonals are 1, 6, 11 and 16. Adding them, we get:

$$1 + 6 + 11 + 16 = 34$$

The numbers in the other diagonal are 4, 7, 10 and 13. On adding these we get:

$$4 + 7 + 10 + 13 = 34$$

And this will also be the sum of the circled numbers.

Special Tips

1. If you are asked to perform the above trick again but with different numbers, you can make a table of consecutive numbers starting from a number other than 1. Then quickly add the numbers of one of the diagonals to get the number you need to predict.

    For example, you can make a table from 11 to 26:

11	12	13	14
15	16	17	18
19	20	21	22
23	24	25	26

    For the prediction sum, just add the numbers of one of the diagonals of the table. In this case, you will get 74.

2. You may also try the trick with larger grids as well, say 5 × 5, and write consecutive numbers in it. The prediction sum of the remaining numbers will always be the sum of the numbers of either of the diagonals.

7

MATHEMAGICAL EYE

I n this trick we will show you how to use your mathemagical eye.

All you need is:
    – 20 objects (you may have similar or different objects)

MAGIC TRICK 8

Step 1
Place 20 objects on the table and turn around so that you cannot see them.

Step 2
Ask your friend or someone from audience to remove at least 1 and a maximum of 10 objects. Hence, the number of objects that remain on table will be 10 or more.

Step 3

Ask that person to add the two digits of the number of objects remaining on the table (e.g. if the number of remaining objects is 17, then the sum is 1 + 7 = 8). Whatever the result, ask them to remove that many objects from the table.

Step 4

Now, ask them or another person to give you some of the remaining objects.

Just by seeing the number of objects given to you, you can tell the number of objects remaining on the table using your mathemagical eye.

MATHS BEHIND THE MAGIC 7

- You started with 20 objects.
- After removing 1 to 10 objects, the number of objects remaining on the table will be between 10 and 19.
- If you add the 2 digits of the remaining number of objects and subtract it from the number itself, you will always get 9, as shown below:

Remaining objects	Sum of the digits	Result
19	1 + 9 = 10	19 − 10 = 9
18	1 + 8 = 9	18 − 9 = 9
17	1 + 7 = 8	17 − 8 = 9
16	1 + 6 = 7	16 − 7 = 9
15	1 + 5 = 6	15 − 6 = 9
14	1 + 4 = 5	14 − 5 = 9
13	1 + 3 = 4	13 − 4 = 9
12	1 + 2 = 3	12 − 3 = 9
11	1 + 1 = 2	11 − 2 = 9
10	1 + 0 = 1	10 − 1 = 9

- Keeping this rule in mind we asked the person to add the digits of the number of objects remaining on the table and then remove that many objects again.
- So, in the last step, when the person gives you some of the objects from the table, you just need to subtract them from 9 to get the final number of objects remaining on the table.

8

MAGICAL WINDOW

This magical trick can be performed with a person of any age group, using some number cards.

All you need is:
- Chart paper or some plain white paper
- A pen
- A cutter

CREATING MAGICAL CARDS

Step 1
To make the game, cut out seven rectangular cards from the paper, of equal size (say 8" × 6").

Step 2
On one card, write the numbers from 1 to 20, as shown in Figure 8.1 below.

MAGICAL CARDS				
1	2	3	4	5
10	9	8	7	6
11	12	13	14	15
20	19	18	17	16
MIND-READER CARD				

Figure 8.1

Step 3

On the remaining 6 cards, cut out the windows (the shaded boxes) in the pattern shown in Figures 8.2 to 8.7 and also write down the numbers in the bottom two rows of the cards.

MAGICAL CARDS				
Magical Windows				
4	7	9	10	16
15	16	18	19	20

Figure 8.2

MAGICAL CARDS				
Magical Windows				
2	5	8	9	11
14	15	17	18	20

Figure 8.3

Figure 8.4   Figure 8.5

Figure 8.6   Figure 8.7

Now the game is ready!

HOW TO PLAY THE TRICK

Step 1
Ask your friend or a volunteer to think of a number from the 'main card' and let them tell you on which of the other 6 cards the number appears in the bottom rows.

Step 2
There will be 3 cards on which it appears. Stack these cards on top of the other and place these on the main card, aligning the edges.

The number your friend thought of will appear in the magical window!

MATHS BEHIND THE MAGIC 8

There are a total of 20 numbers on the main card, i.e. from 1 to 20, and there are 6 mask cards (cards with some cut out windows).

Every number of the main card (i.e. from 1 to 20) is there on exactly 3 cards of these 6 mask cards.

There are 20 different ways of selecting 3 cards out of 6. This can be calculated using the mathematical formula of 'permutation and combination' as follows:

$$^6C_3 = \frac{6!}{(6-3)!3!} = \frac{6 \times 5 \times 4}{3 \times 2} = 20$$

So you can have 20 different numbers shown within the magic window which is unique with each combination of 3 cards.

This happens because the windows are cut in such a pattern so that each combination of 3 cards leaves only a single window uncovered.

9

MYSTERIOUS MAGICAL NUMBERS

In this chapter you will see tricks that will make you exercise your brain like never before. You will get a unique answer at the end of each trick irrespective of the number you pick.

A. FANTASTIC FOUR

1. Start with any whole number and write it out in words.
2. Count the number of characters in its spelling (count spaces and hyphens as well) to get a second number.
3. Count the number of characters in the second number to get a third number.
4. Continue this process until you arrive at a unique number that keeps repeating.

Which magical number is it?

B. A SURPRISING NUMBER

1. Enter 999999 into your calculator.
2. Then divide it by 7.
3. Now throw a dice and multiply the previous result with the number on your dice.
4. Arrange the digits of the product from lowest to highest and write it to form a six-digit number.

What is this number?

C. EVEN, ODD AND MORE

1. Start with any number.
2. Count the number of even digits, the number of odd digits and the total number of digits.
3. Using the above answers, write the digits of new number as: (number of even digits) (number of odd digits) (total number of digits)
4. For the next number, repeat the second step again, i.e. count even, odd and total digits to get another new number.
5. If there are no odd digits or no even digits, write '0' in its place.
6. Repeat steps 2 and 3, and continue until you get a repeating number.

What is the magical repeating number?

D. HAPPY BIRTHDATE

1. Multiply your birthdate (in DDMMYY format) by 8.
2. Add your original number (i.e. your birthdate) to the answer obtained.

3. Add '8' to the result.

4. Now add the individual digits of the result obtained in the previous step. If the sum is more than one digit, take that sum and add up its digits. Continue adding up digits until only one digit is left.

What is the final magical digit?

E. SPECIAL DIVISORS

1. Start with any number greater than 1.

2. Write down all its divisors, including 1 and the number itself.

3. Add each digit of all these divisor(s).

4. Repeat steps 2 and 3 until you get the same number again and again.

What magical number did you get finally?

F. SUBTRACTION SERIES

1. Write any four-digit number with at least two different digits.

2. Rearrange the digits from largest to smallest and write the new number.

3. Rearrange again from smallest to largest (the reverse of step 2) and write it below the previous number.

4. Subtract the two numbers and write down the result, (remember to include leading zeros in both cases so that the number remains in four digits).

5. Keep repeating the above steps (2, 3 and 4) until you arrive at constant magical difference.

What is the magical difference number?

SOLUTIONS

A. FANTASTIC FOUR

The magical number is: **4**.

Example 1:

- Start with any whole number and write its numeral in words:

$$5 \longrightarrow \text{FIVE}$$

- Count the number of characters in its spelling (count spaces and hyphens as well) to get a second number:

$$\text{FIVE} \longrightarrow 4$$

- Count the number of characters in the second number to get the third number:

$$\text{FOUR} \longrightarrow 4$$

Example 2:

Start with **163**.

163 $\longrightarrow$	One hundred and sixty-three
23 $\longrightarrow$	Twenty-three
12 $\longrightarrow$	Twelve
6 $\longrightarrow$	Six
3 $\longrightarrow$	Three
5 $\longrightarrow$	Five
4 $\longrightarrow$	Four

B. A SURPRISING NUMBER

The surprising number is: **124578**.

Example 1:

- Enter 999999 into your calculator.
- Then divide it by 7.

$$999999 \div 7 = 142857$$

- Now throw a dice and multiply the previous result with the number on your dice, say 3.

$$142857 \times 3 = 428571$$

- Arrange the digits of the product from lowest to highest and write it to form a six-digit number.

$$124578$$

Example 2:

$$999999 \div 7 = 142857$$

Let's say the number on dice is 6,

$$142857 \times 6 = 857142$$

Arrange the digits of the product from lowest to highest, we get: 124578

C. EVEN, ODD AND MORE

The magical number is: **123**.

Example 1:

Let's choose **60864127689**,

No. of even digits = 8 (0 is an even number)

No. of odd digits = 3

Total no. of digits = 11

So the new number = **8311**

Now again,

No. of even digits = 1

No. of odd digits = 3

Total no. of digits = 4

So the new number = **134**

Applying recursion,

No. of even digits = 1

No. of odd digits = 2

Total no. of digits = 3

So, the magical answer is **123**.

D. HAPPY BIRTHDATE

The final magical digit is: **8**.

Example 1:

• Multiply your birth date by 8.

Say, 110690 (for 11 June 1990) × 8 = 885520

- Add your original number to the product obtained.

$$885520 + 110690 = 996210$$

- Add 8 to the result.

$$996210 + 8 = 996218$$

- Now add the individual digits of the result obtained in last step.

$$9 + 9 + 6 + 2 + 1 + 8 = 35$$
$$3 + 5 = \mathbf{8}$$

E. SPECIAL DIVISORS

The magical number is: **15**.

Example 1:

Start with any number greater than one, say the number is 20.

- Write down all its divisors, including 1 and itself.

   Divisors of 20 are: 1, 2, 4, 5, 10 and 20

- Add all the digits of these divisor(s).

$$1 + 2 + 4 + 5 + 1 + 0 + 2 + 0 = 15$$

- Repeat steps 2 and 3 until you get the same number again and again.

   Divisors of 15 are: 1, 3, 5, 15
$$1 + 3 + 5 + 1 + 5 = 15$$

F. SUBTRACTION SERIES

The magical difference number is: **6174**.

Example 1:

- Write any four-digit number with at least two different digits:

  1027

- Rearrange the digits from largest to smallest and write the new number:

  7210

- Rearrange again from smallest to largest (or reverse of above) and write it down below the previous number:

  7210

  0127

- Subtract the two numbers and write down the result, (remember to include leading zeros in both cases so that they are all four-digit numbers):

  7210

  − 0127

  7083

- Keep repeating the above steps until you arrive at a constant magical difference.

8730	8532	7641
− 0378	− 2358	− 1467
8352	**6174**	**6174**

The final magical answer is **6174**.
The number 6174 is also known as Kaprekar's constant.

Special Tip

If we take a three-digit number instead of a four-digit one, the magical subtraction result would be *495*.

Try to find the magical subtraction result for a five-digit number.

10

MATHMANIA

This is a cool mind-reading trick, which you can perform even without coming face-to-face with the person, for example, on the phone.

All you need is:
– A paper
– A pen or a pencil
– A calculator

MAGIC TRICK 10

Step 1
Ask your volunteer to write down any four-digit number.

Step 2
Tell them to write the same number again alongside to make it an eight-digit one.

For example, if their number is 4567, it should be written as 45674567.

Step 3
Ask them to divide it by 137.
45674567 ÷ 137 = 333391.

Step 4
This new resulting number should then be divided by the original number.
333391 ÷ 4567 = 73.

Step 5
Now say, 'I can tell you that you have a two-digit number as your answer. Just keep this number in your mind and let us see if I can read it.' Wait for a few seconds before saying, 'Aha! 73 it is . . . Am I right?'

'Aha! 73 it is . . . Am I right?'

MATHS BEHIND THE MAGIC 10

1. When you ask someone to write any four-digit number twice to get an eight-digit number, it is mathematically the same as multiplying your original number by 10001.

$$4567 \times 10001 = 45674567$$

2. The only 'prime' factors of 10001 are 137 and 73, i.e. $137 \times 73 = 10001$, that means

$$4567 \times 137 \times 73 = 45674567$$

3. After Step 1, you asked your volunteer to divide the eight-digit number by 137 and then the resulting number by the original number.

$$\frac{4567 \times 137 \times 73}{137} = 4567 \times 73 = 333391$$

$$\frac{333391}{4567} = \frac{4567 \times 73}{4567} = 73$$

This is the same as:

$$\frac{45674567}{4567} = 10001 \quad \text{and} \quad \frac{10001}{137} = 73$$

So, with the above explanation it is clear why we will always get *73* as the final answer.

Special Tips

- You can make a new trick from this one by asking the participant to write a three-digit number instead of a four-digit one. Say, the number is 123.
- When the participant writes the number twice, it will become a multiple of 1001, i.e. 123123 = 123 × 1001.
- The prime factors of 1001 are 7, 13 and 11, i.e. 1001 = 7 × 13 × 11.
- Now tell your volunteer to divide the six-digit number by 7, the original number and 13. The final answer would be 11.
- While dividing, you can alternatively use any of the two numbers from 7, 13, 11, along with the original number in any sequence and accordingly change the prediction of the final answer.

11

ARITH-MAGIC

This is an amazing trick where you actually lead the other person to the desired result without them even realizing it. You can use this trick in many variations.

All you need is:
  – A paper
  – A pen
  – A calculator

MAGIC TRICK 11

Version 1

1. Ask your volunteer to think of any number, (preferably with two or three digits, so that it's easy to calculate). Tell them to write it on a piece of paper.

2. Then square that number (i.e. multiply the number by itself).

3. Ask them to add the result to the original number.
4. They should now divide the result by the original number.
5. Ask them to add 17 to the result.
6. Tell them to subtract the original number from the result.
7. Finally, they have to divide the result by 3.

If the calculations are correct, the final answer must be 6.
This result stands for any number that you thought of initially.
Now if you want to repeat this trick, bring about a little variation.

Version 2

1. Think of any number and write it down on a piece of paper.
2. Square the number (multiply the number by itself).
3. Add the result to the original number.
4. Divide the result by the original number.
5. To the result, add 19.
6. Subtract the original number from the result.
7. Divide the result by 4.

The answer will always be 5.

Although the volunteer is using their own number as a part of calculations that you are not aware of, you discreetly guide them to the answer you want.

MATHS BEHIND THE MAGIC 11

The first secret of this trick is that the final answer will remain the same irrespective of the number you choose initially, provided you follow the steps in the same sequence.

Step 1
Since you do not know your volunteer's number, replace it with a variable:

$$x$$

Step 2
Square that number (i.e. multiply the number by itself).
$$x \times x = x^2$$

Step 3
Add the result to the original number.
$$x^2 + x$$

Step 4
Divide the result by the original number.
$$\frac{x^2 + x}{x} = \frac{x(x + 1)}{x} = (x + 1)$$

Step 5
To the result, add 17.
$$x + 1 + 17 = x + 18$$

Step 6
Subtract the original number from the result.
$$x + 18 - x = 18$$

Step 7
Divide the result by 3.

$$18 \div 3 = 6$$

So now you know how the final answer is always 6.

Now use a similar calculation method to verify the second version of this trick.

12

GUESSING ONE'S AGE BY THE SIZE OF ONE'S SHOE

Age, weight, height and shoe size are personal information known only to a person or someone close to them. By using the magic of maths in this trick, you can surprise anyone by guessing these details accurately.

All you need is:
  – A paper
  – A pen or a pencil

MAGIC TRICK 12

Ask a volunteer to write down their age on a piece of paper.
Ask them to follow these steps:

1. Multiply the age by 1/5 of 100.

2. Add today's date (i.e. if it is 20 June, add 20).

3. Multiply by 20% of 25.

4. Now add your shoe size.

5. Finally, subtract five times the
    date.

Ask them to tell you the final answer.

Depending on the number of digits
in the answer, you can predict the age
and the shoe size:

The last two digits stand for the shoe size. The remaining digits
tell you their age.

For example, if the final answer is:

- 906: 9 (age), 06 (shoe size)
- 1208: 12 (age), 08 (shoe size)
- 3410: 34 (age), 10 (shoe size)
- 10009: 100 (age), 09 (shoe size)

Special Tip

You may use the trick to guess the height and weight of a
person, or any other two parameters.

HOW TO PLAY THE TRICK

Let's understand the calculation with an example.

Suppose, the person writes down their age as 24 and follows the given steps:

Step 1
Multiply it by 1/5 of 100, i.e. by 20.
$24 \times 20 = 480$

Step 2
Add today's date. Let's say today is the 15th day of the month, then, $480 + 15 = 495$

Step 3
Multiply by 20% of 25, i.e. by 5.
$495 \times 5 = 2475$

Step 4
Now, add your shoe size; say the size is 7, then,
$2475 + 7 = 2482$

Step 5
Subtract 5 times today's date from it. In this case, subtract 5×15, i.e. 75.

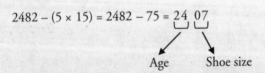

$$2482 - (5 \times 15) = 2482 - 75 = \underbrace{24}_{\text{Age}}\ \underbrace{07}_{\text{Shoe size}}$$

Then the last two digits of the final answer will always tell the size of the person's shoe and the remaining digit(s) will tell the person's age.

MATHS BEHIND THE MAGIC 12

Let's follow the steps using variables a and b, where a stands for age and b stands for shoe size.

- Multiply the age by 20 : $a \times 20 = 20a$

- Add today's date : $20a + 15$
  (assuming today's date is 15)

- Multiply by 5 : $(20a + 15) \times 5$
  $= 100a + (15 \times 5)$

- Add the shoe size : $100a + (15 \times 5) + b$

- Subtract 5 times today's date : $100a + (15 \times 5) + b - (15 \times 5)$

- Answer : $100a + b$

From the above calculations, it is clear that

1. The place value of age in the final answer will always be hundreds or more as it is multiplied by 100.
2. As the shoe size is never more than two digits, it will always be in the ones and tens place in the final answer.

13

MAGICAL SYMBOLS

A dd to your performance skills with this different kind of trick.

All you need is:
– A chart of magical symbols

MAGIC TRICK 13

Step 1
Ask a person from the audience to think of a two-digit number between 20 and 99.

Step 2
Ask them to add the two digits together.

Step 3
Subtract this sum from their original number.

10	♣	11	○	12	♪	13	✳	14	☽
15	□	16	■	17	♦	18	☺	19	♥
20	✳	21	♣	22	●	23	□	24	■
25	♫	26	☽	27	☺	28	♦	29	☾
30	♠	31	♥	32	☾	33	♫	34	♣
35	○	36	☺	37	♠	38	☽	39	□
40	■	41	●	42	✳	43	♠	44	○
45	☺	46	☽	47	♣	48	■	49	✳
50	♦	51	♫	52	☽	53	○	54	☺
55	☹	56	♦	57	☹	58	●	59	●
60	●	61	○	62	♥	63	☺	64	♠
65	♠	66	□	67	○	68	♣	69	□
70	☽	71	♣	72	☺	73	♠	74	♫
75	♫	76	✳	77	□	78	♦	79	☹
80	●	81	☺	82	♣	83	☾	84	■
85	☾	86	♠	87	■	88	♫	89	♦
90	☺	91	♣	92	☹	93	●	94	♥
95	■	96	♫	97	□	98	○	99	☺

Step 4

Display the copy of the magical symbols chart shown above and ask the person to find the resulting number on the symbols chart and focus on the symbol beside that number.

Step 5

After a few seconds, hide the chart.

Correctly guess that the corresponding symbol is: ☺.

MATHS BEHIND THE MAGIC 13

Let's understand the working using an example.

Suppose a participant picks 37.
Adding both the digits, we get $3 + 7 = 10$.
Subtracting this sum from the original number, we get
$37 - 10 = 27$.
Symbol corresponding to 27 is ☺.
You will always get those numbers that are represented by ☺.

Let's see how:

1. Take the digits of our two-digit number as a and b, where a is at tens place and b is at ones place.

2. Since a is in the tens place, it should be multiplied by 10 and the number will be written as:

$$10a + b$$

3. When we add the two digits, we get:

$$a + b$$

4. Subtracting this sum from our original number, we get :

$$(10a + b) - (a + b) = 9a$$

5. That means, the final answer will always be a multiple of 9. So, very smartly, in our symbol chart, we have put the same symbol (☺) for all multiples of 9, i.e. 18, 27, 36 and so on.

Special Tip

You can prepare more symbol charts, each with a different symbol used for the multiples of 9. That way, you can play the same trick on the same audience again and again till they notice the secret.

14

MAGIC WITH DICE

Dice are not just useful for playing board games, but also for performing magic tricks. For this one, we will use three regular dice.

MAGIC TRICK 14

Step 1
Give your friend or some spectator three dice and turn around so that you aren't facing them.
Ask them to roll the three dice without telling you the outcome.

Step 2
Ask them to choose one of the three numbers.

Step 3
Tell them to multiply the selected number by 2.

Step 4
Ask them to add 5 to the new number.

Step 5
Tell them to multiply the result of Step 4 by 5 and add the number of the second dice to it.

Step 6
Instruct them to multiply the new result by 10 and add the number of the third dice to it.

Step 7
Now tell the person to subtract 125 from the new number.

Ask that person to tell you the final total.

Now pretend to summon your magical powers to guess the numbers on the dice.

Here comes the magic!

Mentally, just subtract 125 from the final total to get a three-digit number. Surprise everyone by revealing these three digits as the three numbers of the dice rolled.

MATHS BEHIND THE MAGIC 14

1. Let us consider the outcomes of the three dice as a, b and c.

2. Choose one of these three numbers, suppose a, as the first number.

3. Multiplying the number by 2 it becomes,

$$2a$$

4. Adding 5 results in

$$2a + 5$$

5. Multiplying it by 5 gives us

$$(2a + 5) \times 5$$

$$10a + 25$$

6. Adding the second number:

$$10a + 25 + b$$

$$Or$$

$$(10a + b) + 25$$

7. Multiplying it by 10 gives us

$$100a + 10b + 250$$

8. Adding the remaining third number, we get:

$$100a + 10b + 250 + c$$

9. Subtracting '125' from it will result in:

$$100a + 10b + c + 125$$

10. Now again you have to subtract '125' mentally, from the result told by the spectator. You will get the final number as

$$100a + 10b + c$$

Thus you will always get a three-digit number with the first digit as a, second digit as b and third digit as c.

15

CALCULATOR MAGIC

This trick will convince people you are a mathemagician whose mind is as fast as a calculator. Everyone will wonder how you can perform complex calculations in seconds.

All you need is:
- A paper
- A pen or a pencil
- A calculator

MAGIC TRICK 15

Step 1
Ask a person from the audience to volunteer and request them to type any number between 1 and 900 on the calculator. Tell the person to keep this a secret. (If your calculator can display more than ten digits, the user can also pick a number greater than 900.)

Let's assume that the person types 891 on the calculator.
Now tell them to follow these steps.

Step 2
Multiply this number by 3.
891 × 3 = 2673

Step 3
Multiply the result by 7.
2673 × 7 = 18711

Step 4
Multiply the result by 37.
18711 × 37 = 692307

Step 5
Then multiply the result by 11.
692307 × 11 = 7615377

Step 6
Multiply the result by 13.
7615377 × 13 = 98999901

Ask the person to tell you the final answer.

Now, just by looking at this number you will be able to guess the number the volunteer chose in Step 1, i.e. 891.

MATHS BEHIND THE MAGIC 15

1. In this trick, we have multiplied the number by 3, 7, 37, 11 and 13. The product of these numbers is:

    $$3 \times 7 \times 37 \times 11 \times 13 = 111111$$

2. So, we are actually making the person multiply the number by 111111.

3. The final answer will have digits in a particular pattern. It could be one of the following patterns:

    RRRRRR
    F RRRRR L
    F RRRR B L
    FF RRR BB L

    Let me explain what these letters stand for.

    R: Repeat—these are the repeating digits, located in the centre of the number.

    F: First—these are located at the beginning of the number right before the 'repeat' digits. There can be one, two or no 'first' digits.

    L: Last—this digit is located at the end of the final answer. There can be at most one digit that can be considered the 'last'.

    B: Between—these come between the 'repeat' and 'last' digits. There can be one, two or no digits between 'repeat' and 'last'.

4. Let's see how these F, R, B, L patterns in the final answer will eventually lead us to the original number.

a) Subtract B (between) from R (repeat). Make sure that the number of digits is the same for both. That means if there is only one number between 'repeat' and 'last', deduct it from only one digit of the repeated number, i.e. R.

b) Subtract the difference obtained in the above step from the entire 'first' digits (F or FF.)

c) Prefix the new answer to L (last) digit to get the original number.

To understand the procedure better, let us take few examples.

Example 1:

The person chooses 891.

After following the procedure of the trick, the final result would be

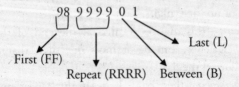

To get the original number, simply do the following:
- 9 – 0 = 9 (i.e. R – B)
- 98 – 9 = 89 (i.e. FF – answer of Step 1)
- Attach 89 to 1 to get 891 (i.e. answer of Step 2 and L digit)

Example 2:

The person chooses 555.

After following the procedure, the final result would be 61666605.

So, in this resulting number:

First digits (FF) = 61

Repeat digits (RRRR) = 6666

Between digit (B) = 0

Last digit (L) = 5

To get the original number, simply do the following:

- 6 – 0 = 6 (i.e. R – B)
- 61 – 6 = 55 (i.e. FF – answer of Step 1)
- Attach 55 to 5 to get 555 (i.e. answer of Step 2 and L digit)

Example 3:

The person chooses 548.

After following the procedure, the final result would be 60888828.

So, in this resulting number:

First digits (FF) = 60

Repeat digits (RRRR) = 8888

Between digit (B) = 2

Last digit (L) = 8

To get the original number, simply do the following:

- 8 – 2 = 6 (i.e. R – B)
- 60 – 6 = 54 (i.e. FF – answer of Step 1)
- Attach 54 to 8 to get 548 (i.e. answer of Step 2 and L digit)

Example 4:

The person chooses 127.

After following the procedure, the final result would be 14111097.

So, in this resulting number:
First digits (FF) = 14
Repeat digits (RRR) = 111
Between digit (B) = 09
Last digit (L) = 7

To get the original number, simply do the following:

- 11 – 09 = 2 (i.e. R – B)
- 14 – 2 = 12 (i.e. FF – answer of Step 1)
- Attach 12 to 7 to get 127 (i.e. answer of Step 2 and L digit)

Example 5:

The person chooses 6.

After following the procedure, the final result would be 666666.

So, in this resulting number:
Repeat digits (RRRRRR) = 666666

As the answer has only 'repeat' digits after being multiplied by 111111, the original number must be a single number, i.e. 6 in the case.

Let us summarize the above process of getting the original number from the answer using the F, R, B, L digits pattern:

a) If the final answer has only 'repeat' digits, i.e. repeated numbers that means the original number is that single number. For example, if the final answer is 666666, the original number is 6.

b) If the 'between' digit does not exist, attach the 'first', i.e. F, digit to the left of the 'last', or L, digit to get the original number. Say, the final answer is '2555553', then the original number would be '23'.

c) If the 'between' digit(s) exist, subtract them from the same number of digits in the 'repeat'.

- Subtract this difference obtained in the above step from the 'first' digits, F or FF.
- Prefix the newly obtained digit(s) to the L digit to get the original number.

16

CALENDAR TRICKS

A calendar is a good example of how maths is an inbuilt part of our everyday lives. In this chapter, we will explore some mind-boggling patterns of numbers present in a calendar. You can use the calendar of any month or any year.

Let's take a look at January 2017:

January 2017						
Sun	**Mon**	**Tue**	**Wed**	**Thu**	**Fri**	**Sat**
1	2	3	4	5	6	7
8	9	10	11	12	13	14
15	16	17	18	19	20	21
22	23	24	25	26	27	28
29	30	31				

Magical Pattern 1:

Select any row of numbers (i.e. horizontal lines) and add its first and the last number. Let's take first row of the above calendar as shown below:

January 2017						
Sun	**Mon**	**Tue**	**Wed**	**Thu**	**Fri**	**Sat**
1	2	3	4	5	6	7
8	9	10	11	12	13	14
15	16	17	18	19	20	21
22	23	24	25	26	27	28
29	30	31				

Adding the first and the last number of the row, we get:

$$1 + 7 = 8$$

The result '8' is double of the middle number between 1 and 7, i.e. double of 4.

Similarly,

$$2 + 6 = 8$$

(i.e. double of middle number between 2 and 6)

That shows that *the middle number is always the average.*

Also when you sum up all the numbers of this row, you will get:

$$1 + 2 + 3 + 4 + 5 + 6 + 7 = 28$$

The result is 7 times the middle number 4 (i.e. $7 \times 4 = 28$), as the middle number is the average number of the row.

Try and check the above pattern with other rows. Which means the total of the second row should be 77 (i.e. $7 \times 11 = 77$) and the total of the third row should be 126 (i.e. $7 \times 18 = 126$).

Magical Pattern 2:

January 2017						
Sun	**Mon**	**Tue**	**Wed**	**Thu**	**Fri**	**Sat**
1	2	3	4	5	6	7
8	9	10	11	12	13	14
15	16	17	18	19	20	21
22	23	24	25	26	27	28
29	30	31				

Choose any section of the calendar that includes a 3 × 3 square grid, as highlighted in the above image.

Now, add the three numbers of the middle row of the grid, then add the three numbers of the middle column of the grid and also add the three numbers that appear on the right diagonal and left diagonal separately, of the selected grid, as shown below:

$$9 + 10 + 11 = 30$$
$$3 + 10 + 17 = 30$$
$$4 + 10 + 16 = 30$$
$$2 + 10 + 18 = 30$$

The middle row, middle column, both diagonals add up to the same number!

Try and check the above pattern by taking 3 × 3 grid in other sections of the calendar, as highlighted in the below images:

January 2017						
Sun	Mon	Tue	Wed	Thu	Fri	Sat
1	2	3	4	5	6	7
8	9	10	11	12	13	14
15	16	17	18	19	20	21
22	23	24	25	26	27	28
29	30	31				

January 2017						
Sun	Mon	Tue	Wed	Thu	Fri	Sat
1	2	3	4	5	6	7
8	9	10	11	12	13	14
15	16	17	18	19	20	21
22	23	24	25	26	27	28
29	30	31				

Magical Pattern 3:

January 2017						
Sun	Mon	Tue	Wed	Thu	Fri	Sat
1	2	3	4	5	6	7
8	9	10	11	12	13	14
15	16	17	18	19	20	21
22	23	24	25	26	27	28
29	30	31				

Select any section of the calendar that includes a 3 × 3 square grid, as highlighted in the above image. In the above grid you can see that '13' is the middle number. So, if you add the side numbers to it you will always get double of 13, i.e. 26, as shown below:

$$6 + 20 = 26$$
$$12 + 14 = 26$$
$$5 + 21 = 26$$
$$7 + 19 = 26$$

So, it shows that *the middle number is the average of all the nine numbers of the grid.*

Thus, it gives us a special trick to sum up all the numbers of the grid.

Multiply the middle number by total numbers in the grid (i.e. 9), and we will get the sum of all the numbers present in the grid, as shown below:

$$5 + 6 + 7 + 12 + 13 + 14 + 19 + 20 + 21 = 117$$

This is same as $13 × 9 = 117$

Try the above trick of finding the sum directly by using other different 3 × 3 grids.

Special Tip

You can surprise your friends using the above formula by asking them to choose any 3 × 3 grid of your calendar and then compete with them in finding the total of all the numbers of the selected grid.

Magical Pattern 4:

January 2017						
Sun	**Mon**	**Tue**	**Wed**	**Thu**	**Fri**	**Sat**
1	2	3	4	5	6	7
8	9	10	11	12	13	14
15	16	17	18	19	20	21
22	23	24	25	26	27	28
29	30	31				

This time, select a rectangle of 20 numbers, i.e. 5 × 4 rectangular grid.

You can get the sum of all the 20 numbers in the grid in a few seconds. The trick is to add the smallest and the largest number in the grid and then multiply it by 10.

So, the sum of the numbers in above grid would be:

$$(2 + 27) \times 10 = 290$$

Amazing, isn't it? Try the above trick with other such 5 × 4 rectangles and amaze everyone.

MATHS BEHIND THE MAGIC 16

The magical patterns in a calendar exist because the numbers are in a special maths sequence, known as Arithmetic Progression (AP). An AP is a sequence of numbers with a fixed difference between any two consecutive numbers. So using the properties of AP we can clearly understand the secret of the patterns discussed above.

In a 3 × 3 grid of a calendar, consecutive rows have a difference of 7 and consecutive columns have a difference of 1. For diagonals, it is 6 and 8 (or –6 and –8, depending on whether you count downwards or upwards).
Three consecutive terms in any arithmetic sequence can be written as a, $a+d$, $a+2d$.

Then, the average $\dfrac{[a+(a+2d)]}{2}$ of the outer two numbers is equal to '$a+d$', which is the middle term.

Similarly, using the properties of AP, we can understand that the formula given above in *Magical Pattern 4* for a 5 × 4 grid are as follows:

Let's consider the first number of the grid as n, then all the numbers in the grid can be written in the following pattern:

n	$n+1$	$n+2$	$n+3$	$n+4$
$n+7$	$n+8$	$n+9$	$n+10$	$n+11$
$n+14$	$n+15$	$n+16$	$n+17$	$n+18$
$n+21$	$n+22$	$n+23$	$n+24$	$n+25$

Now, sum of all the numbers in this grid
$= n + n+1 + n+2 + n+3 + n+4 + n+7 + n+8 + n+9 + n+10 + n+11 + n+21 + n+22 + n+23 + n+24 + n+25$
$= 20n + 250$
$= 10(2n + 25)$
$= 10[n + (n + 25)]$
$= 10(\text{smallest number in the grid} + \text{largest number in the grid})$

FUN WITH NUMBERS

17

CREATIVITY OF RAMANUJAN

Srinivasa Ramanujan is undoubtedly one of the greatest Indian mathematicians who contributed significantly to the field. He had a great knack of finding patterns in numbers and could apply his mathematical bend of mind to any situation.

In the *Journal of the Indian Mathematical Society*, he once gave this equation for the readers to solve:

$$\sqrt{1 + 2\sqrt{1 + 3\sqrt{1 + 4\sqrt{1 + 5\sqrt{1 + 6\ldots}}}}} = ?$$

For the next three issues of the journal, i.e. about six months, he waited for someone to come up with the solution, but no one responded. Everyone thought it was too difficult to solve this infinitely nested radical problem. The editor of the journal thought the equation was incorrect. But to their surprise, Ramanujan revealed that the answer of this equation was simply '3'.

They were astonished when Ramanujan told them that he created this problem when he first learnt about square roots. He gave the following solution for the equation:

$$3 = \sqrt{9}$$

$$= \sqrt{1 + 8}$$

$$= \sqrt{1 + 2 \times 4}$$

$$= \sqrt{1 + 2\sqrt{16}}$$

$$= \sqrt{1 + 2\sqrt{1 + 15}}$$

$$= \sqrt{1 + 2\sqrt{1 + 3 \times 5}}$$

$$= \sqrt{1 + 2\sqrt{1 + 3\sqrt{25}}}$$

$$= \sqrt{1 + 2\sqrt{1 + 3\sqrt{1 + 24}}}$$

$$= \sqrt{1 + 2\sqrt{1 + 3\sqrt{1 + 4 \times 6}}}$$

$$= \sqrt{1 + 2\sqrt{1 + 3\sqrt{1 + 4\sqrt{36}}}} \ldots$$

It's amazing to think that a single-digit number can be represented in such a complex way.

Similar to this exercise, the following chapter, 'Gymnastics with Numbers', will encourage you to use numbers in different ways and represent them innovatively.

18

GYMNASTICS WITH NUMBERS

Over the years, we have shared many number-based activities with more than 20,000 teachers, who have in turn used them while teaching their students. These activities encourage you to think of the right mathematical operation to use in each scenario, thus making you confident of solving other maths problems and creating a question for desired answers.

The beauty of these activities is that they are equally enjoyed by everyone, be it a ten-year-old child, a parent or a teacher.

A. GYMNASTICS WITH '4':

In this activity we will form all the numbers using only number '4'.

Rules to follow:

- Write numbers from 1 to 12 as a combination of only *four 4s* (i.e. the number '4' is to be used *exactly four times*, neither less nor more).

- You can use any mathematical operation(s) to get your number, (like +, −, ×, ÷, etc.). For example, number '1' can be written as $\left(\frac{44}{44}\right)$ or $\left(\frac{4}{4} + 4 - 4\right)$, which means multiple combinations are possible, but you need to give only one combination for each number.
- You can also concatenate (form a series of) numbers (e.g. 44 and 444).
- You can use decimal (.4), square root ($\sqrt{\ }$), factorial (!), etc.

Answers to some numbers are already given here. Try your hand at finding the remaining ones:

$1 = \dfrac{44}{44}$

$2 =$

$3 = \dfrac{(4 + 4 + 4)}{4}$

$4 =$

$5 =$

$6 =$

$7 =$

$8 = \left(\dfrac{4 \times 4}{4}\right) + 4$

$9 =$

$10 =$

$11 =$

$12 =$

Remember to use the rule of BODMAS and proper brackets in your solutions.

For answers turn to page 93.

Special Tip

This activity is like a puzzle. The interesting part is that, you don't have to stop at 12, you can easily go till 100 or even beyond using the number 4 exactly four times.

For more answers of forming numbers up to 1000, using four 4s visit our website: www.aditisinghal.com

B. GYMNASTICS WITH '5':

In this activity we will form all the numbers using only the number '5'.

Rules to follow:

- Write numbers from 1 to 12 as a combination of only *five 5s* (i.e. the number '5' is to be used exactly five times, neither less nor more).
- You can use any mathematical operations to get your number (like +, −, ×, ÷, etc.).
- For example, number '1' can be written as

$$\left[\left(\frac{55}{5}\right) - 5 - 5\right] \text{ or } \left(\frac{5 + \sqrt{5 \times 5}}{5 + 5}\right).$$

- You can also concatenate numbers (e.g. 55 and 555)
- You can use decimal (.5), square root ($\sqrt{\ }$), factorial (!), etc.

Answers to some numbers are already given here, try finding the remaining ones

1 $= \left(\dfrac{55}{5}\right) - 5 - 5$

2 $=$

3 $=$

4 $=$

5 $=$

6 $= \left(\dfrac{5}{5}\right) \times 5 + \left(\dfrac{5}{5}\right)$

7 $=$

8 $=$

9 $=$

10 $=$

11 $=$

12 $=$

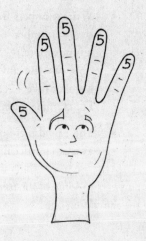

 Remember to use the rule of BODMAS and proper brackets in your solutions.

For answers, turn to page 94.

C. GYMNASTICS WITH '6':

In this activity we will form all the numbers using only number '6'.

Rules to follow:

- Write numbers from 1 to 12 as a combination of only *six 6s* (i.e. number '6' is to be used exactly six times, neither less nor more.)
- You can use any mathematical operations to get your number (like +, −, ×, ÷, etc.).
- For example, number '1' can be written as $\left(\dfrac{6}{6} \times \dfrac{6}{6} \times \dfrac{6}{6} \right)$.
- You can also concatenate numbers (e.g. 66 and 666).
- You can use decimal (.6), square root ($\sqrt{\ }$), factorial (!), etc.

Answers to some of the numbers are already given here, try finding the remaining ones:

$1 \quad = \left(\dfrac{6}{6} \times \dfrac{6}{6} \times \dfrac{6}{6} \right)$

$2 \quad =$

$3 \quad =$

$4 \quad =$

$5 \quad =$

$6 \quad =$

$7 \quad =$

$8 \quad = \dfrac{6}{6} \times 6 + \dfrac{6+6}{6}$

9 =

10 =

11 =

12 =

 Remember to use the rule of BODMAS and proper brackets in your solutions.

For answers, turn to page 96.

D. GYMNASTICS WITH '3':

In this activity we will form all numbers using only the number '3'.

Rules to follow:

- Write numbers from 1 to 12 using only *three 3s* (i.e. the number '3' is to be used exactly three times, neither less nor more).
- You can use any mathematical operations to get your number (like +, −, ×, ÷, etc.)
- For example, number '1' can be written as $\dfrac{\sqrt{3} \times \sqrt{3}}{3}$
- You can also concatenate numbers (e.g. 33 and 333),
- You can use decimal (.3), square root ($\sqrt{}$), factorial (!), etc.

Answers to some of the numbers are already given here, try finding the remaining ones:

1 $= \dfrac{\sqrt{3} \times \sqrt{3}}{3}$

2 =

3 =

4 =

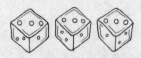

5 =

6 =

7 $= \dfrac{3}{.3} - 3$

8 =

9 =

10 =

11 =

12 =

 Remember to use the rule of BODMAS and proper brackets in your solutions.

For answers, turn to page 97.

For more answers of forming numbers, visit our website: www.aditisinghal.com

Solutions for gymnastics with number '4':

$1 \quad = \quad \left(\dfrac{44}{44}\right)$

$2 \quad = \quad \left(\dfrac{4}{4}\right) + \left(\dfrac{4}{4}\right)$

$3 \quad = \quad \left(\dfrac{4+4+4}{4}\right)$

$4 \quad = \quad 4\left(4-4\right) + 4$

$5 \quad = \quad \left(\dfrac{(4 \times 4) + 4}{4}\right)$

$6 \quad = \quad \left(\dfrac{4+4}{4}\right) + 4$

$7 \quad = \quad \left(\dfrac{44}{4}\right) - 4$

$8 \quad = \quad \left(\dfrac{4 \times 4}{4}\right) + 4 \text{ or } \left(\dfrac{4}{4}\right)(4+4)$

$9 \quad = \quad \left(\dfrac{4}{4}\right) + 4 + 4$

$10 \quad = \quad \left(\dfrac{44}{4.4}\right)$

$11 \quad = \quad \left(\dfrac{4}{.4}\right) + \left(\dfrac{4}{4}\right) \text{ or } \dfrac{44}{\sqrt{4} \times \sqrt{4}}$

$12 \quad = \quad \left(\dfrac{44 + 4}{4}\right)$

$13 \quad = \quad 4! - \dfrac{44}{4}$

$14 \quad = \quad 4 \times \left(4 - .4\right) - .4$

$15 \quad = \quad \dfrac{44}{4} + 4$

$16 \quad = \quad 4 \times 4 \times \dfrac{4}{4}$

$17 \quad = \quad \dfrac{4}{4} + (4 \times 4)$

$18 \quad = \quad (44 \times .4) + .4$

$19 \quad = \quad 4! - 4 - \dfrac{4}{4}$

$20 \quad = \quad 4\left(\dfrac{4}{4} + 4 \right)$

Solutions for gymnastics with number '5':

$1 \quad = \quad \left(\dfrac{55}{5} \right) - 5 - 5$

$2 \quad = \quad \left(\dfrac{5+5}{5} \right) + 5 - 5$

$3 \quad = \quad \left(\dfrac{5+5}{5} \right) + \left(\dfrac{5}{5} \right)$

$4 \quad = \quad \left(\dfrac{5+5+5+5}{5} \right)$

$5 \quad = \quad \left(\dfrac{5}{5} \right) \times \left(\dfrac{5}{5} \right) \times 5$

$6 \quad = \quad \left(\dfrac{5}{5} \right) \times 5 + \left(\dfrac{5}{5} \right)$

$7 \quad = \quad \left(\dfrac{5}{5} \right) + \left(\dfrac{5}{5} \right) + 5$

$8 \quad = \quad 5 + 5 - \left(\dfrac{5+5}{5} \right)$

$9 \quad = \quad 5 + 5 - 5^{(5-5)} \text{ OR } \dfrac{(5 \times 5) - 5}{5} + 5$

$10 \quad = \quad (5 \times 5) - 5 - 5 - 5$

$11 \quad = \quad \left(\dfrac{55}{5}\right) + 5 - 5$

$12 \quad = \quad \left(\dfrac{55}{5}\right) + \left(\dfrac{5}{5}\right)$

$13 \quad = \quad \left(\dfrac{5!}{5+5}\right) + \left(\dfrac{5}{5}\right)$

$14 \quad = \quad \left(\dfrac{5! - (5 \times 5)}{5}\right) - 5$

$15 \quad = \quad \left(5 + \sqrt{5}\right) \left(5 - \sqrt{5}\right) - 5$

$16 \quad = \quad \sqrt{5! + \dfrac{5}{5}} + \sqrt{5 \times 5}$

$17 \quad = \quad \dfrac{55 + 5}{5} + 5$

$18 \quad = \quad \dfrac{5!}{5} - 5 - \dfrac{5}{5}$

$19 \quad = \quad \dfrac{5!}{5} - 5 + 5 - 5$

$20 \quad = \quad \dfrac{5}{.5} \times \dfrac{5+5}{5} \quad \text{OR} \quad \dfrac{5! - (5 \times 5) + 5}{5}$

Note: 5! = 5 × 4 × 3 × 2 × 1 = 120

Solutions for gymnastics with number '6':

$$1 \quad = \quad \left(\frac{6}{6} \times \frac{6}{6} \times \frac{6}{6} \right)$$

$$2 \quad = \quad \frac{6}{6} + \frac{6}{6} \times \frac{6}{6}$$

$$3 \quad = \quad \frac{6}{6} + \frac{6}{6} + \frac{6}{6}$$

$$4 \quad = \quad \frac{6+6}{6} + \frac{6+6}{6}$$

$$5 \quad = \quad 6 + \frac{6}{6} - \frac{6+6}{6}$$

$$6 \quad = \quad \sqrt{6 + 6 + 6 + 6 + 6 + 6}$$

$$7 \quad = \quad \frac{6}{6} \times \frac{6}{6} + \sqrt{6 \times 6}$$

$$8 \quad = \quad \frac{6}{6} \times 6 + \frac{6+6}{6}$$

$$9 \quad = \quad 6 + 6 - \left(\frac{6+6+6}{6} \right)$$

$$10 \quad = \quad 6 + \left(6 - \frac{6}{6} \right) - \frac{6}{6}$$

$$11 \quad = \quad 6 + \left(6 - \frac{6}{6} \right) \times \frac{6}{6}$$

$$12 \quad = \quad 6 + 6 + 6 + 6 - 6 - 6$$

$$13 \quad = \quad (6 + 6) + \left(\frac{6}{6} \times \frac{6}{6} \right)$$

$$14 \quad = \quad 6 + 6 + \frac{6}{6} + \frac{6}{6}$$

15 $\quad=\quad 6 + 6 + \dfrac{6+6+6}{6}$

16 $\quad=\quad 6 + 6 + 6 - \dfrac{6+6}{6}$

17 $\quad=\quad 6 + 6 + 6 - 6^{6-6}$

18 $\quad=\quad 6 + 6 + 6 \times 6^{6-6}$

19 $\quad=\quad 6 + 6 + 6 + 6^{6-6}$

20 $\quad=\quad 6 + 6 + 6 + \dfrac{6+6}{6}$

Solutions for gymnastics with number '3':

1 $\quad=\quad \dfrac{\sqrt{3} \times \sqrt{3}}{3}$

2 $\quad=\quad 3 - \dfrac{3}{3}$

3 $\quad=\quad 3 \times \dfrac{3}{3}$

4 $\quad=\quad 3 + \dfrac{3}{3}$

5 $\quad=\quad \dfrac{3!}{3} + 3$

6 $\quad=\quad (3 \times 3) - 3 \text{ or } 3! \times \dfrac{3}{3}$

7 $\quad=\quad 3! + \dfrac{3}{3}$

8 $\quad=\quad \left(\dfrac{3!}{3}\right)^{3} \text{ or } 3! + \dfrac{3!}{3}$

9	=	$3 + 3 + 3$
10	=	$\dfrac{\sqrt{3} \times \sqrt{3}}{.3}$
11	=	$\dfrac{33}{3}$
12	=	$3! + 3 + 3$
13	=	$\dfrac{3}{.3} + 3$
14	=	$3 \times \left(\sqrt{3} + 3\right)$
15	=	$(3 \times 3!) - 3 \ \text{ or } \ 3! + (3 \times 3)$
16	=	$\dfrac{(3 + 3)!!}{3}$
17	=	$\dfrac{3!}{.3} - 3$
18	=	$(3 + 3) \times 3$
19	=	$\dfrac{(3!)!!}{3} + 3$
20	=	$\dfrac{3 + 3}{.3}$

Note: $3! = 3 \times 2 \times 1 = 6$

$6!! = 6 \times 4 \times 2 = 48$

$n!! = n \times (n - 2) \times (n - 4) \ldots \times 2,$ *where n is even*

$n!! = n \times (n - 2) \times (n - 4) \ldots 3 \times 1,$ *where n is odd*

19

NEW YEAR NUMBERS

Over the years, while interacting with the teachers, students and others who attend our maths workshops, we have found out that the key difference between those who have a good understanding of the subject and those who don't is in the way they deal with numbers. It is not that the latter have less knowledge, but they are more dependent on procedures and try to memorize facts instead of understanding the concepts. They fear using numbers flexibly. For example, 31 – 6 is easier to calculate when we think of it as 30 – 5, but the less confident ones merely count backwards from 31.

So to develop number sense and flexibility with numbers, we are sharing one more version of the activity shared in the last chapter, i.e. 'Gymnastics with Numbers'. Earlier we created numbers using only one particular digit, say 4, 5, 6, etc. In this chapter we use *four digits* of the current or any special year to make all the numbers, e.g. year 2017 is made up of digits 2, 0, 1 and 7. This way, students will get a new perspective on how maths is a part of their daily life.

Rules to follow:

- Write numbers from 1 to 12 as a combination of only four digits present in the current year (i.e. if the year is '2017', the digits to be used are 2, 0, 1 and 7 only).
- You can use each of the four digits only once.
- You can use any mathematical operations to get your number (like +, −, ×, ÷, etc.).
- You can also concatenate (form a series of) numbers (e.g. 21 and 721).
- You can use decimals (.2), exponents, square roots ($\sqrt{\ }$), factorial (!), Int ([]) (i.e. greatest integer function), etc.
- Remember to use the rule of BODMAS and proper brackets in your solutions.

Answers to some of the year numbers are already given here. Try finding the remaining ones:

YEAR 2018	
Numbers	**Solution**
1	$(2 - 1) + (8 \times 0)$
2	
3	$2 + 1 + (8 \times 0)$
4	
5	
6	
7	
8	
9	$8 + 1 + 2 \times 0$
10	$2 + 8 + 1 - 0!$
11	
12	

Grid: 1

YEAR 2017	
Numbers	**Solution**
1	
2	$(2 \times 1) + (7 \times 0)$
3	
4	
5	
6	
7	
8	$(2 \times 0) + 1 + 7$
9	
10	
11	
12	$(2 + 1)! + 7 - 0!$

Grid: 2

Note: 0! = 1

YEAR 2001	
Numbers	**Solution**
1	1^{200}
2	
3	
4	
5	
6	
7	$(2 + 1)! + 0! + 0$
8	$10 - 2 + 0$
9	
10	
11	
12	$10 + 2 + 0$

Grid: 3

YEAR 2000	
Numbers	**Solution**
1	
2	$2 + 0 + 0 + 0$
3	$2 + 0! + 0 + 0$
4	
5	
6	
7	
8	
9	
10	$\dfrac{20}{(0!+0!)}$
11	
12	$(0! + 0! + 0!)! \times 2$

Grid: 4

YEAR 1999	
Numbers	**Solution**
1	
2	
3	
4	$\sqrt{9} + 1^{99}$
5	
6	
7	

YEAR 1995	
Numbers	**Solution**
1	
2	
3	$\sqrt{9} \times 1^{95}$
4	
5	
6	
7	

8	$\sqrt{9}+\sqrt{9}+\sqrt{9}-1$
9	9×1^{99}
10	
11	
12	

Grid: 5

8	$5+\sqrt{9} \times 1^{9}$
9	$5+\sqrt{9}+1^{9}$
10	
11	
12	

Grid: 6

YEAR 1990	
Numbers	Solution
1	
2	
3	
4	
5	
6	$\sqrt{9}+\sqrt{9} \times 1^{0}$
7	
8	
9	9×1^{90}
10	$19-9+0$
11	
12	

Grid: 7

YEAR 1947	
Numbers	Solution
1	
2	
3	
4	4×1^{97}
5	$4+1^{97}$
6	
7	
8	
9	
10	$9+1^{47}$
11	
12	

Grid: 8

Special Tip

You can make this activity more interesting by doing it on the birthday of a child using his or her year of birth or while discussing some special historic event.

For more answers of forming numbers for other years visit our website: www.aditisinghal.com

SOLUTIONS

YEAR 2018	
Numbers	**Solution**
1	$(2 - 1) + (8 \times 0)$
2	$(2 \times 1) + (8 \times 0)$
3	$2 + 1 + (8 \times 0)$
4	$8 \div 2 + (1 \times 0)$
5	$8 \div 2 + 1 + 0$
6	$8 - 2 + 0 \times 1$
7	$(8 - 1) + 0 \times 2$
8	$(2 + 1) \times 0 + 8$
9	$8 + 1 + 2 \times 0$
10	$2 + 8 + 1 - 0!$
11	$2 + 1 + 8 + 0$
12	$2 + 1 + 8 + 0!$

Grid: 1

YEAR 2017	
Numbers	**Solution**
1	$(2 - 1) + (7 \times 0)$
2	$(2 \times 1) + (7 \times 0)$
3	$2 + 1 + (7 \times 0)$
4	$7 - 2 - 1 - 0$
5	$7 \div 1 - 2 + 0$
6	$7 + 1 - 2 + 0$
7	$(2 + 1) \times 0 + 7$
8	$(2 \times 0) + 1 + 7$
9	$7 + 2 + 1 \times 0$
10	$2 + 0 + 1 + 7$
11	$2 + 1 + 7 + 0!$
12	$(2 + 1)! + 7 - 0!$

Grid: 2

Note: 0! = 1

YEAR 2001		YEAR 2000	
Numbers	**Solution**	**Numbers**	**Solution**
1	1^{200}	1	$2 - 0! + 0 + 0$
2	$2 + (10 \times 0)$	2	$2 + 0 + 0 + 0$
3	$2 + 1 + 0 + 0$	3	$2 + 0! + 0 + 0$
4	$2 + 1 + 0! + 0$	4	$2 + 0! + 0! + 0$
5	$2 + 1 + 0! + 0!$	5	$2 + 0! + 0! + 0!$
6	$(2 + 1)! + 0 + 0$	6	$(0! + 0! + 0!) \times 2$
7	$(2 + 1)! + 0! + 0$	7	$(2 + 0!)! + 0! + 0$
8	$1\,0 - 2 + 0$	8	$2^{(0! + 0! + 0!)}$ or $(0! + 0! + 0!)! + 2$
9	$(0! + 0! + 1)^2$	9	$(0! + 0! + 0!)^2$
10	$10 + (2 \times 0)$	10	$\dfrac{20}{(0! + 0!)}$
11	$10 + 2 - 0!$	11	int(sqrt(sqrt(sqrt((20+0-0!)!))))
12	$10 + 2 + 0$	12	$(0! + 0! + 0!) \times 2$

Grid: 3   *Grid: 4*

YEAR 1999		YEAR 1995	
Numbers	**Solution**	**Numbers**	**Solution**
1	$19 - 9 - 9$	1	1^{995}
2	$\sqrt{9} - 1^{99}$	2	$(19 - 9) \div 5$
3	$\sqrt{9} \times 1^{99}$	3	$\sqrt{9} \times 1^{95}$
4	$\sqrt{9} + 1^{99}$	4	$\sqrt{9} + 1^{95}$
5	$\sqrt{9} + \dfrac{9}{9} + 1$	5	5×1^{99}
6	$\sqrt{9} \times \left(\dfrac{9}{9} + 1\right)$	6	$5 + 1^{99}$
7	$\left(\sqrt{9}\right)! + \left(\dfrac{9}{9} \times 1\right)$ or $\sqrt{9} + \sqrt{9} + 1^9$	7	$5 + \sqrt{9} - 1^9$
8	$\left(\sqrt{9}\right)! + \left(\dfrac{9}{9} + 1\right)$ or $\sqrt{9} + \sqrt{9} + \sqrt{9} - 1$	8	$5 + \sqrt{9} \times 1^9$
9	9×1^{99}	9	$5 + \sqrt{9} + 1^9$
10	$9 + 1^{99}$	10	$5 + (\sqrt{9})! - 1^9$
11	$9 + 1 + \dfrac{9}{9}$	11	$5 + (\sqrt{9})! \times 1^9$
12	$\left(\sqrt{9}\right)! + \sqrt{9} + \sqrt{9} \times 1$ or $\left(\sqrt{9} + \sqrt{9}\right) \times \left(\sqrt{9} - 1\right)$	12	$5 + (\sqrt{9})! + 1^9$

Grid: 5   *Grid: 6*

YEAR 1990		YEAR 1947	
Numbers	**Solution**	**Numbers**	**Solution**
1	1^{990}	1	1^{947}
2	$1^9 + 9^0$	2	$\sqrt{4} \times 1^{97}$
3	$\sqrt{9} \times 1^{90}$	3	$4 - 1^{97}$
4	$\sqrt{9} + 1^{90}$	4	4×1^{97}
5	$\sqrt{9} + \sqrt{9} - 1 + 0$	5	$4 + 1^{97}$
6	$\sqrt{9} + \sqrt{9} \times 1^0$	6	$(4 + 9 - 7) \times 1$
7	$\sqrt{9} + \sqrt{9} + 1 + 0$	7	$4 + 9 - 7 + 1$
8	$(\sqrt{9})! + \sqrt{9} - 1 + 0$	8	$4 \times (9 - 7) \times 1$
9	$9 + 1^{90}$	9	$4 \times (9 - 7) + 1$
10	$19 - 9 + 0$	10	$9 + 1^{47}$
11	$(\sqrt{9})! + (\sqrt{9})! - 1^0$	11	$9 + (7 - 4) - 1$
12	$(\sqrt{9})! + (\sqrt{9})! \times 1^0$	12	$(9 \times 1) + 7 - 4$

Grid: 7   *Grid: 8*

20

MAGIC SQUARES

Magic squares have fascinated people for ages. Since ancient times, these magic squares have been a part of various rituals in different parts of the world. In India, you can find them in Ganesha Yantra, Lakshmi Yantra, etc., as symbols that are believed to increase wealth.

The oldest magic square of the fourth order was found inscribed in Khajuraho, India, dating back to the eleventh or twelfth century. This magic square is also known as the diabolic or panmagic square.

In ancient times, people believed that magic squares could prevent certain diseases. Certain tribes would wear a magic square made of silver around the neck as a talisman against plague.

Magic squares are square grids with a special arrangement of numbers in them. These squares are magical because every row, column and diagonal adds up to the same number, known as the magical sum or constant.

Figure 20.1 shows a fourth-order (i.e. 4 × 4) magic square, with 64 as the magical constant.

44	1	12	7
11	8	43	2
5	10	3	46
4	45	6	9

Figure 20.1

The magical constant, 64, is obtained not just by adding the numbers in any column, row or diagonal but also by adding four numbers from the square in many different ways.

Some of the combinations of four numbers, in this magic square, adding to 64 are shown below:

44	1	12	7
11	8	43	2
5	10	3	46
4	45	6	9

64   64   64   64

Figure 20.2

44	1	12	7	64
11	8	43	2	64
5	10	3	46	64
4	45	6	9	64

Figure 20.3

Figure 20.4

Figure 20.5

The sum of each of the four columns (Figure 20.2), four rows (Figure 20.3) and two diagonals (Figure 20.4 and Figure 20.5) is 64, as highlighted in the figures above. Some of other possible combinations are as follows:

Figure 20.6

Figure 20.7

Figure 20.8

Figure 20.9

44	1	12	7
11	8	43	2
5	10	3	46
4	45	6	9

Figure 20.10

44	1	12	7
11	8	43	2
5	10	3	46
4	45	6	9

Figure 20.11

44	1	12	7
11	8	43	2
5	10	3	46
4	45	6	9

Figure 20.12

44	1	12	7
11	8	43	2
5	10	3	46
4	45	6	9

Figure 20.13

44	1	12	7
11	8	43	2
5	10	3	46
4	45	6	9

Figure 20.14

44	1	12	7
11	8	43	2
5	10	3	46
4	45	6	9

Figure 20.15

44	1	12	7
11	8	43	2
5	10	3	46
4	45	6	9

Figure 20.16

44	1	12	7
11	8	43	2
5	10	3	46
4	45	6	9

Figure 20.17

44	1	12	7
11	8	43	2
5	10	3	46
4	45	6	9

Figure 20.18

44	1	12	7
11	8	43	2
5	10	3	46
4	45	6	9

Figure 20.19

44	1	12	7
11	8	43	2
5	10	3	46
4	45	6	9

Figure 20.20

44	1	12	7
11	8	43	2
5	10	3	46
4	45	6	9

Figure 20.21

44	1	12	7
11	8	43	2
5	10	3	46
4	45	6	9

Figure 20.22

44	1	12	7
11	8	43	2
5	10	3	46
4	45	6	9

Figure 20.23

44	1	12	7
11	8	43	2
5	10	3	46
4	45	6	9

Figure 20.24

44	1	12	7
11	8	43	2
5	10	3	46
4	45	6	9

Figure 20.25

Try to find other combinations or visit our website, www.aditisinghal.com, for more such magic squares.

HOW TO CONSTRUCT A MAGIC SQUARE

To construct a magic square with a magical constant between 22 and 99, use the following grid as reference:

$x-20$	1	12	7
11	8	$x-21$	2
5	10	3	$x-18$
4	$x-19$	6	9

Figure 20.26

In this 4×4 magic square, there are twelve fixed numbers and four other numbers that are calculated using a variable x, where x is the magical constant for which you are creating a magic square. In the above example (in Figure 20.1), the magical constant (x) is 64.

Now try to create a magic square with the constant of 36, using the above pattern.

Special Tip

If you have to make two magic squares of two different numbers for the same audience, you can use the following grid also, so that audience does not recognize the pattern of fixed numbers.

13	$x - 30$	7	10
6	11	12	$x - 29$
8	5	$x - 28$	15
$x - 27$	14	9	4

Figure 20.27

You can even create birthday magic squares for people around you. These squares are customized according to a person's date of birth, so it's a great way to make someone feel special.

Formula for Creating a Birthday Magic Square

A	B	C	D
D + 1	C − 1	B − 3	A + 3
B − 2	A + 2	D + 2	C − 2
C + 1	D − 1	A + 1	B − 1

Figure 20.28

Think of the birth date of the person as AA-BB-CCDD, where AA is the date, BB is the month, CC is the first two digits of the year and DD is the last two digits of the year.

For example, the birthday magic square of 02-10-1997 is as follows:

02	10	19	97
98	18	7	5
8	4	99	17
20	96	3	0

Figure 20.29

The magical constant of the above magic square is 128.

The sum of each of the four columns (Figure 20.30), four rows (Figure 20.31) and two diagonals (Figure 20.32 and 20.33) is 128 as highlighted in the figures below.

02	10	19	97
98	18	7	5
8	4	99	17
20	96	3	9

Figure 20.30

02	10	19	97
98	18	7	5
8	4	99	17
20	96	3	9

Figure 20.31

02	10	19	97
98	18	7	5
8	4	99	17
20	96	3	9

128

Figure 20.32

02	10	19	97
98	18	7	5
8	4	99	17
20	96	3	9

Figure 20.33

You can find more combinations in the above magic square as discussed earlier in the chapter.

In a birthday magic square, sometimes some numbers may repeat in a grid, but we can still get the magical constant in them, e.g. if the date is 03-03-2003, the number 3 is repeated thrice in the first row itself .

Special Tip

Using the above formula, you can create a magic square for any special date.

21

MATHS TAMBOLA

In this chapter, we are introducing a maths game that can be played in parties, classrooms or in small get-togethers. Playing this game will not only improve your concentration and mental calculations but it is a lot of fun too. We call it 'maths tambola'. It is similar to the game Tambola (also known as Bingo or Housie). The important difference is that instead of calling a number directly, say 44, the caller may say '11 × 4' or '11 × 2 × 2' or '88 ÷ 2' or '35 + 9', etc.

Materials required:

- Tambola tickets
- Calling-number game sheet (given in this chapter)
- A pen/pencil/toothpick for each players to strike out the called numbers in their tickets

Rules:

- Give one Tambola ticket to each participant/player.

- Using the game sheet, the caller needs to say the expression given corresponding to the number he wants to call.
- If the number arrived at after doing the mental calculation exists on a player's ticket, the player has to strike it out.
- Once a player gets a particular winning combination,* he or she has to claim it immediately.
- Caller has to verify the winner by matching the struck-out numbers on the ticket with the called-out numbers.
- Game ends when all the Full Houses are successfully claimed.

*The winning combinations are:

- Early 5: The first ticket with five struck-out numbers
- First/Second/Third Row: The first ticket with all numbers struck out in a particular row
- Corner with Star: The first ticket with all four corner numbers and the central number struck out (first and last numbers of top and bottom rows along with the third number of the middle row)
- Full House/First House: The first ticket with all its numbers struck out
- Second House: The second ticket with all its numbers struck out and so on

Sample ticket:

5				49		63	75	80
		28	34		52	66	77	
6	11				59	69		82

GAME SHEET

Actual No.	1	2	3	4	5	6	7	8	9	10
Called No.	17/17	6/3	$\sqrt{9}$	2*2	10/2	$\sqrt{36}$	21/3	32/4	3*3	100/10
Actual No.	11	12	13	14	15	16	17	18	19	20
Called No.	99/9	72/6	7+6	2*7	5*3	4*4	8+9	9*2	23-4	5*4
Actual No.	21	22	23	24	25	26	27	28	29	30
Called No.	7*3	13+9	14+9	6*4	5*5	13*2	9*3	7*4	15+14	6*5
Actual No.	31	32	33	34	35	36	37	38	39	40
Called No.	22+9	8*4	3*11	17*2	5*7	9*4	23+14	19*2	13*3	4*10
Actual No.	41	42	43	44	45	46	47	48	49	50
Called No.	22+19	3*2*7	24+19	11*2*2	9*5	23*2	39+8	12*4	7*7	5*10
Actual No.	51	52	53	54	55	56	57	58	59	60
Called No.	17*3	2*2*13	34+19	2*3*9	5*11	7*2*4	3*19	29*2	59/1	12*5
Actual No.	61	62	63	64	65	66	67	68	69	70
Called No.	43+18	31*2	3*3*7	4*4*4	13*5	2*3*11	48+19	4*17	23*3	5*14
Actual No.	71	72	73	74	75	76	77	78	79	80
Called No.	52+19	4*18	37+36	2*37	5*15	4*19	7*11	3*2*13	52+27	16*5
Actual No.	81	82	83	84	85	86	87	88	89	90
Called No.	9*9	2*41	74+9	4*3*7	5*17	2*43	78+9	4*2*11	28+61	9*10

According to the participants, you may change the arithmetic expressions of the original numbers as per your choice.

22

IMPROVING CONCENTRATION USING NUMBERS

In any kind of work we do, be it painting, playing a sport or studying, concentration plays an important role. All successful artists, sports persons, scientists, writers and other creative performers have very high levels of concentration. Here, we are going to use 'counting' as a tool to help us improve our concentration and attention span.

Rules:

1. Count the number of symbols or images in a block without actually touching the images or any other part of the block.
2. Do not try to count using fingers or any equipment.
3. Maximum time allowed for counting images in a block is three minutes.
4. Continue counting the number of symbols in a block till you get the same answer for three consecutive times, then move on to the next block.

Block 1

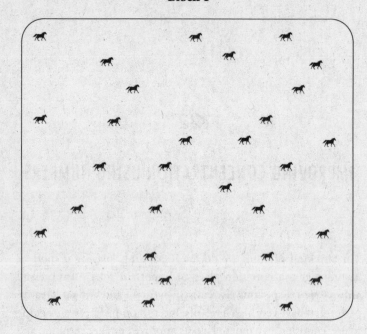

Block 2

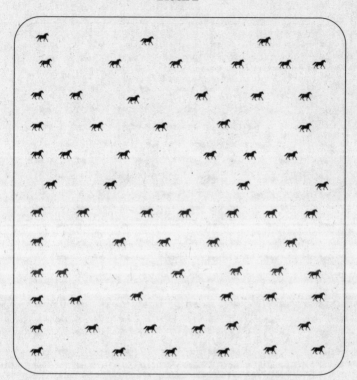

Block 3

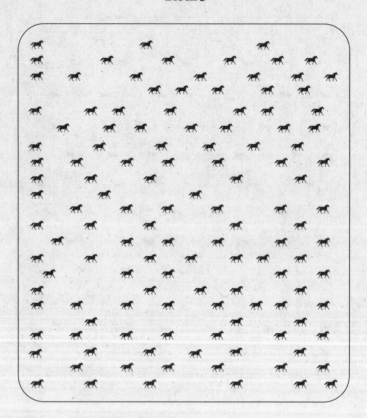

Practising counting on these blocks improves your concentration, reading speed as well as problem-solving skills.

23

MATHS MNEMONICS

A mnemonic is a memory aid, such as an abbreviation, rhyme or mental image that helps you remember something. In this chapter, we are introducing some maths mnemonics in the form of acronyms, sentences and various other associations which will help you to remember maths facts and formulae.

1. **Arithmetic (Spelling)**
    Mnemonic: **A R**at **I**n **T**he **H**ouse **M**ay **E**at **T**he **I**ce **C**ream.
    The first letter of each word of the sentence collectively forms the word 'ARITHMETIC'.

2. **Greater Than or Less Than (> or <)**
    How can you tell which symbol stands for greater than or less than?
    Mnemonic: The symbol '>' or '<' can be seen as alligator's open mouth.
    'The hungry alligator will open its mouth wider towards the larger number.'

3. Metric Units in Order

- Kilo
- Hecto
- Deca
- Units *(metre, litre, gram)*
- Deci
- Centi
- Milli

Mnemonic: **K**ing **H**enry **D**ied **U**nexpectedly **D**rinking **C**hocolate **M**ilk.

OR

King Henry Danced (Merrily/Lazily/Grandly) Drinking Chocolate Milk.

For the standard units, you can insert 'merrily' (for metre), 'lazily' (for litre) or 'grandly' (for gram).

4. Mode and Median

(i) **Mode**:

The *mode* is the value that occurs the *most*.

'**MO**de' and '**MO**st', first two letters in both the words are common.

OR

The **MODE** is the **M**ost **O**ccurring **D**ata **E**ntity.

(ii) **Median**:

The *median* splits the data down the *middle*, like the median strip on a road.

5. Simple Interest Formula

Interest = Principle × Rate × Time

I = PRT

Read as '**I** am going to **PaRT**y'.

6. Speed, Distance and Time

Distance = Speed × Time

D = ST

Remember it as **DuST:** 'When I was driving at a high speed, my car got covered with DuST.'

7. Value of Pi (π)

Count the number of letters in each word:

(i) **Pi (π) to 7 decimal places**

May I have a large container of coffee?

3.1415926

(ii) **Pi (π) to 10 decimal places**

May I have a large container of coffee ready for today?

3.1415926535

8. Area and Circumference of Circle

(i) Area of a Circle

Apple pie are square: $A = \pi \times r^2$

(ii) Circumference of a Circle

Cherry pie delicious: $C = \pi \times d$

9. Complementary and Supplementary Angles

(i) A corner is a 90° angle, and a Corner is Complementary. A straight angle is 180°, and Supplementary angles are Straight angles.

(ii) In the alphabet, the letter 'C' for complementary comes before the letter 'S' for supplementary, and in the number line 90 comes before 180.

(iii) The word complementary has one p, the word supplementary has two p's. We can take one p to represent 90° and two p's to represent 180°.

10. Trigonometry Function Properties

Which trigonometry functions are positive in each quadrant?

All in Quadrant I

Sine in Quadrant II

Tangent in Quadrant III

Cosine in Quadrant IV

This sequence can be memorized using the abbreviation 'ASTC'.

Mnemonics to remember 'ASTC':

A Smart Trigo Class

All Students Take Calculus

All Stores Take Cash

To know more maths mnemonics and to learn the detailed procedure of creating your own, refer to our book *How to Memorize Anything*.